Science

Written by John Farndon
Illustrated by Julian Baker

This is a Parragon Book
This edition published in 2002

Parragon
Queen Street House
4 Queen Street
Bath BA1 1HE, UK

ISBN: 0-75259-299-8

Printed in China

Produced by Miles Kelly Publishing Ltd

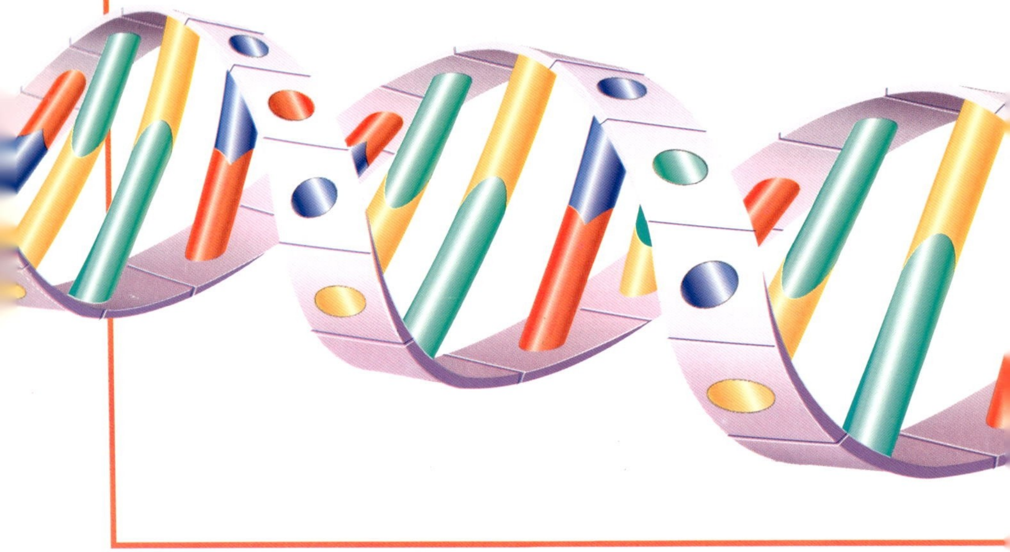

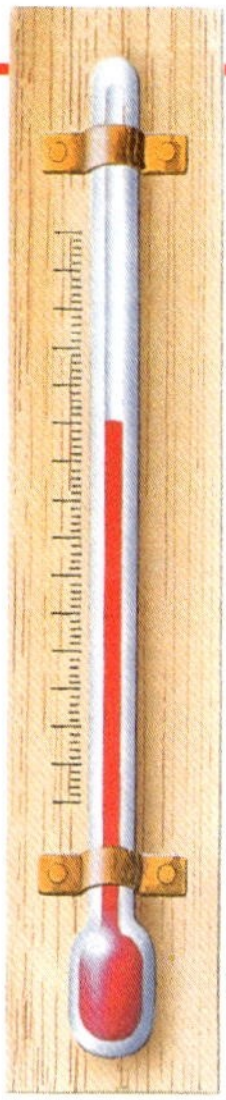

Contents

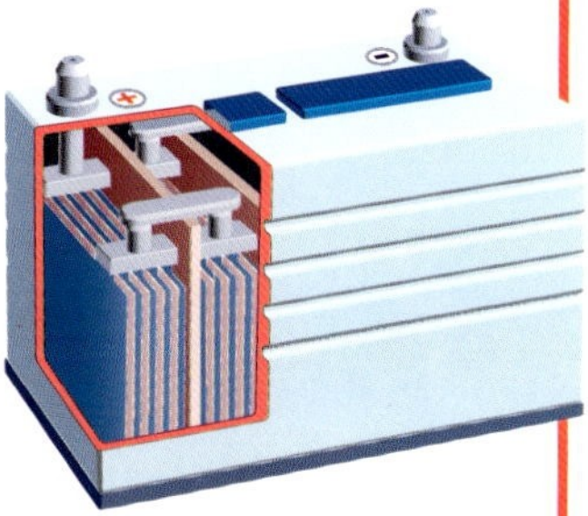

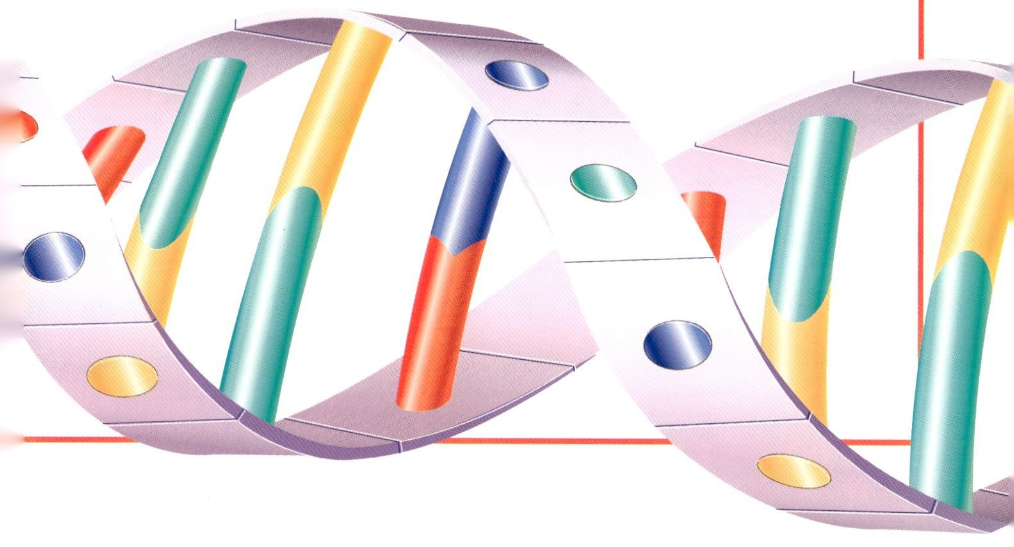

What are solids?

SUBSTANCES CAN BE EITHER SOLID, LIQUID OR GAS – THE THREE 'STATES OF MATTER'. Substances move from one state to another when they are heated or cooled – boosting or reducing the energy of the particles they are made of. In solids, particles are locked together, so solids have a definite shape and volume. In liquids, particles move around a bit, so liquids can flow into any shape – but stay the same volume. In gases, particles zoom about all over the place, so gases spread out to fill containers of any size or shape. When a substance is normally a liquid but turns into a gas, this is called a vapour.

What is a plasma?

A plasma is the rare fourth state of matter. It occurs only when a gas becomes so hot its particles break up. This happens inside the Sun and stars and in lightning, and in gas neon tubes. Plasmas are good conductors of electricity.

When do things freeze?

Things freeze from liquid to solid when they reach the freezing point, which is the same as melting point. Most substances get smaller when they freeze as the particles pack closer together. Water gets bigger as it turns to ice, which is why frozen pipes burst in winter.

What substance has the highest melting point?

The metal with the highest melting point is tungsten, which melts at 3,420°C (6,188°F). But the highest melting point of any substance belongs to carbon, which melts at 3,530°C (6,386°F).

What substance has the lowest freezing point?

Mercury has the lowest freezing point of any metal –38.87°C (–37.96°F). Helium has the lowest freezing point of all substances – –272.2°C (–457.96°F), less than 1° above absolute zero.

When do things boil?

Things boil from liquid to gas when they reach boiling point, which is the maximum temperature a liquid can reach. For water this is 100°C (212°F). An increase in pressure increases boiling point, which is why pressure cookers allow things to cook at higher temperatures.

Water as solid, liquid and gas

Solids do not keep their shape completely. The ice in glaciers can flow very slowly.

When do things melt?

Things melt from solid to liquid on reaching a temperature called the melting point. Each substance has its own melting point. Water's is 0°C (32°F); lead's is 327.5°C (621.5°F).

Thunderclouds

Large thunderclouds are made from water droplets and ice crystals.

What happens in evaporation and condensation?

EVAPORATION HAPPENS WHEN A LIQUID IS WARMED UP AND CHANGES TO A VAPOUR. Particles at the liquid's surface vibrate so fast they escape altogether. Condensation happens when a vapour is cooled down and becomes liquid. Evaporation and condensation take place not only at boiling point, but also at much cooler temperatures.

What is pressure?
Pressure is the amount of force pressing on something. Air pressure is the force with which air presses. The force comes from the bombardment of the moving air particles. The more particles there are, and the faster they are moving, the greater the pressure.

How does pressure change?
If you squeeze a gas into half the space, the pressure doubles (as long as the temperature stays the same). This is Boyle's law. If you warm a gas up, the pressure rises in proportion (as long as you keep it the same volume). This is the Pressure law.

Clouds form when rising air gets so cold that the water vapour it contains condenses into water droplets.

What is an atom?

ATOMS ARE WHAT EVERY SUBSTANCE IS MADE OF. ATOMS ARE THE SMALLEST recognizable bit of any substance. They are so small that they are visible only under extremely high-powered microscopes – you could fit two billion atoms on the full stop at the end of this sentence. Yet atoms are largely composed of empty space – empty space dotted with even tinier clouds of energy called sub-atomic particles.

What is the nucleus?
Most of an atom is empty space, but right at its centre is a very tiny area that is densely packed with particles much bigger than electrons. This is the nucleus, and it usually contains two kinds of nuclear particle – neutrons with no electrical charge, and protons with a positive electrical charge (opposite to the negative charge of electrons).

How big are atoms?
Atoms are about a ten millionth of a millimetre across and weigh 100 trillionths of a trillionth of a gram. The smallest atom is hydrogen; the biggest is meitnerium. (Since they are so small, atoms are measured in terms of 'moles', which is a quantity of the substance containing the same number of atoms as 12 grams of a form of carbon called Carbon 12.)

What are electrons?
Electrons are the very tiny electrically charged particles that whizz round inside an atom. They were discovered by the English physicist J.J. Thomson (1856–1940) in 1879 during some experiments with cathode ray tubes. (Computer and TV screens are cathode ray tubes, and cathode rays are actually streams of electrons.)

What is a molecule?
Quite often, atoms cannot exist by themselves, and must always join up with others – either of the same kind, or with other kinds to form chemical compounds. A molecule is the smallest particle of a substance that can exist on its own.

What is an ion?
An ion is an atom that has either lost one or a few electrons, making it positively charged (cation) or gained a few, making it negatively charged (anion). Ions usually form when substances dissolve in a liquid.

Inside a proton

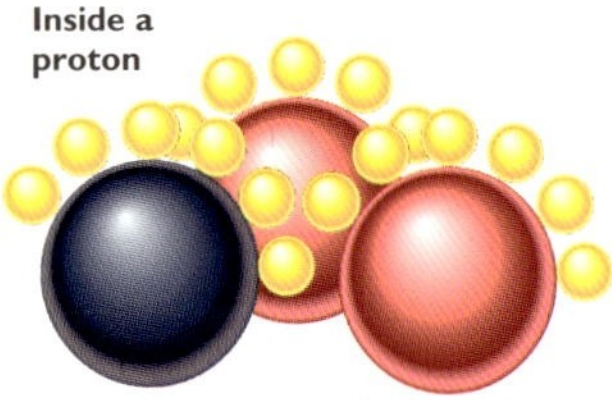

Protons may be made of even smaller particles – quarks joined by gluons.

What holds atoms together?
Electrons are held to the nucleus by electrical attraction – because they have an opposite electrical charge to the protons in the nucleus. The particles of the nucleus are held together by a force called the strong nuclear force.

What are electron shells?

ELECTRONS BEHAVE AS IF THEY ARE STACKED AROUND THE NUCLEUS AT different levels, like the layers of an onion. These levels are called shells, and there is room for only a particular number of electrons in each shell. The number of electrons in the outer shell determines how the atom will react with other atoms. An atom with a full outer shell, like the gas argon, is unresponsive. An atom with room for one or more extra electrons in its outer shell, like oxygen, is very reactive.

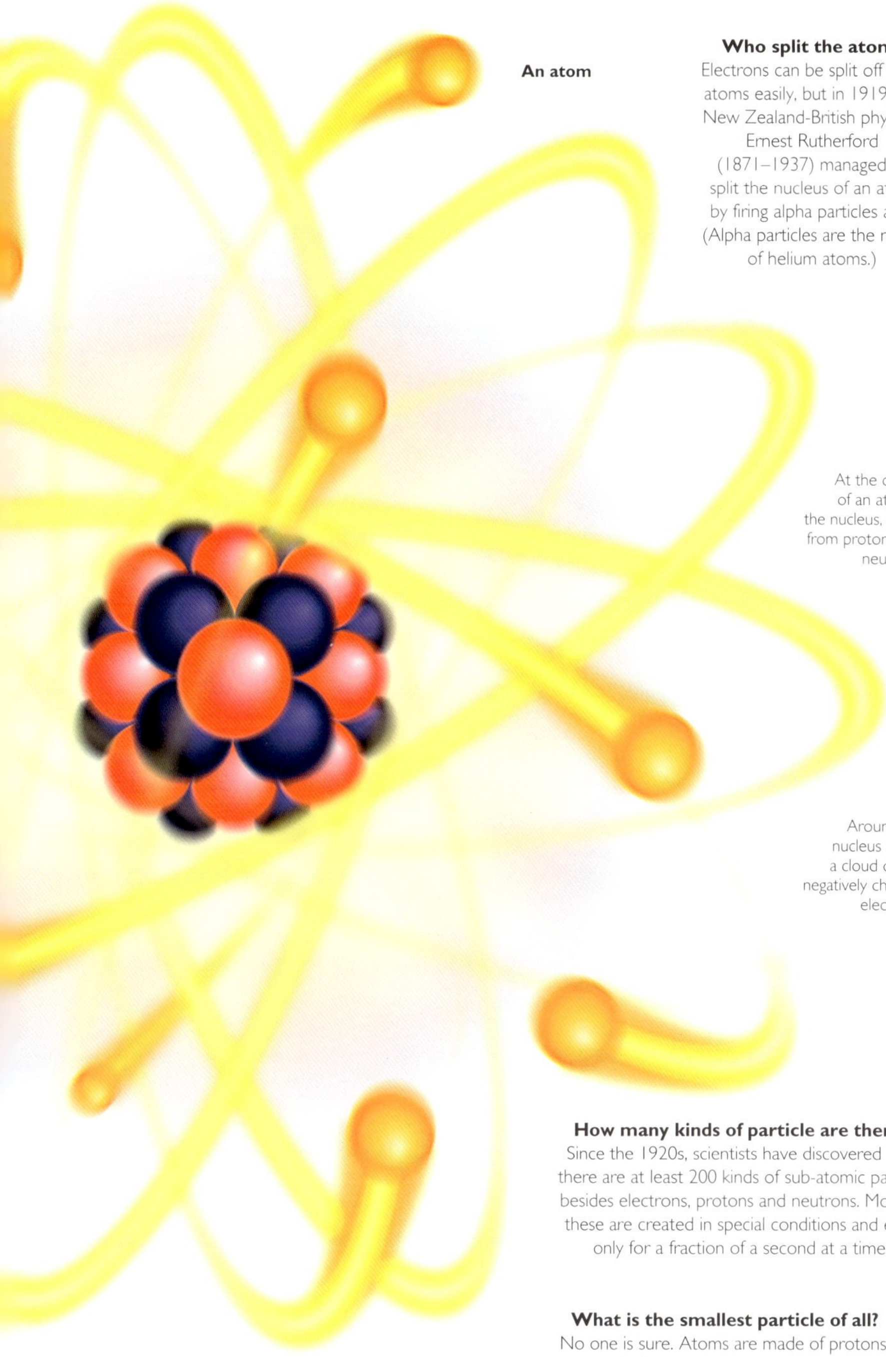

An atom

At the centre of an atom is the nucleus, made from protons and neutrons.

Around the nucleus whirls a cloud of tiny negatively charged electrons.

Who split the atom?
Electrons can be split off from atoms easily, but in 1919, the New Zealand-British physicist Ernest Rutherford (1871–1937) managed to split the nucleus of an atom by firing alpha particles at it. (Alpha particles are the nuclei of helium atoms.)

How many kinds of particle are there?
Since the 1920s, scientists have discovered that there are at least 200 kinds of sub-atomic particle besides electrons, protons and neutrons. Most of these are created in special conditions and exist only for a fraction of a second at a time.

What is the smallest particle of all?
No one is sure. Atoms are made of protons, neutrons and electrons. In turn, these could be made of even tinier particles – quarks and leptons. But one day, we might discover even smaller particles....

How many elements are there?

New elements are discovered every so often, but the total number identified so far is 112.

Fluorine

What are noble gases?

Group 0 is the furthest right-hand column of the periodic table. This group is called the noble gases, because they have full-up outer electron shells and so nobly stay aloof from any reaction with 'base' metals or any other substance. They are sometimes called inert gases.

Why are some elements reactive?

Elements are reactive if they readily gain or lose electrons. Elements on the left of the periodic table, called metals, lose electrons very easily – the further left they are, the more reactive they are. So Group I metals (called the alkali metals) including sodium, potassium and francium are very reactive.

What is the heaviest element?

The heaviest is hahnium. It has 105 protons and 157 neutrons in its nucleus. The atomic mass of hahnium is 262.

What are the transition metals?

Transition metals are the metals in the middle of the periodic table, such as chromium, gold and copper. They are generally shiny and tough, but easily shaped. They conduct electricity well and have high melting and boiling points.

What is a metal?

Most people can recognize a metal. It is hard, dense and shiny, and goes 'ping' when you strike it with something else made of metal. It also conducts both electricity and heat well. Chemists define a metal as an electropositive element, which basically means that metals easily lose negatively charged electrons. It is these lost, 'free' electrons that make metals such excellent conductors of electricity.

Silver

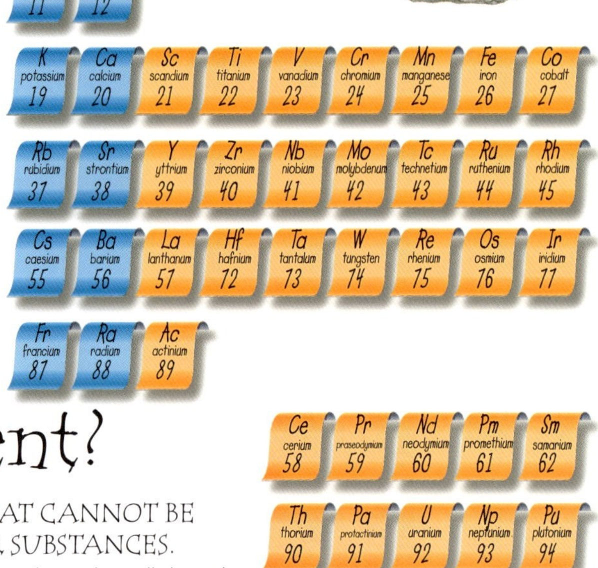

What is an element?

IT IS A SUBSTANCE THAT CANNOT BE SPLIT UP INTO OTHER SUBSTANCES.

Water is not an element because it can be split into the gases oxygen and hydrogen. Oxygen and hydrogen are elements because they cannot be split. Every element has its own atomic number. This is the number of protons in its nucleus, which is balanced by the same number of electrons.

Uranium

What is the periodic table?

ALL THE ELEMENTS CAN BE ORDERED ACCORDING TO THEIR PROPERTIES, forming a chart called the periodic table. Columns are called groups, rows are called periods. Elements in the same group have the same number of electrons in the outer shell of their atoms and similar properties.

Why is carbon so special?
Carbon is the most friendly element in the Universe. With four electrons in the outer shell of its atom (and so four gaps), carbon atoms link very readily with other atoms.

Who discovered radium?
The Polish-French physicist Marie Curie (1867–1934), born Marya Sklodowska, is the only woman to have won two Nobel prizes – one in 1903 for her part in the discovery of radioactivity, and one in 1911 for her discovery of the elements polonium and radium.

Copper

								He helium 2
			B boron 5	C carbon 6	N nitrogen 7	O oxygen 8	F fluorine 9	Ne neon 10
			Al aluminium 13	Si silicon 14	P phosphorus 15	S sulphur 16	Cl chlorine 17	Ar argon 18
Ni nickel 28	Cu copper 29	Zn zinc 30	Ga gallium 31	Ge germanium 32	As arsenic 33	Se selenium 34	Br bromine 35	Kr krypton 36
Pd palladium 46	Ag silver 47	Cd cadmium 48	In indium 49	Sn tin 50	Sb antimony 51	Te tellurium 52	I iodine 53	Xe xenon 54
Pt platinum 78	Au gold 79	Hg mercury 80	Ti thalium 81	Pb lead 82	Bi bismuth 83	Po polonium 84	At astatine 85	Rn radon 86

What is atomic mass?
Atomic mass is the 'weight' of one whole atom of a substance – which is of course very tiny! It includes all the particles in the atom – protons, neutrons and electrons.

Sulphur

What are the lanthanides?
The lanthanides are a group of 15 elements in the middle of the periodic table that take their name from lanthanum. They are all shiny silvery metals and often occur naturally together. They all have two electrons in their outer electron shells. This makes them chemically similar – they are all very reactive.

Eu europium 63	Gd gadolinium 64	Tb terbium 65	Dy dysprosium 66	Ho holmium 67	Er erbium 68	Tm thulium 69	Yb ytterbium 70	Lu lutetium 71
Am americium 95	Cm curium 96	Bk berkelium 97	Cf californium 98	Es einsteinium 99	Fm fermium 100	Md mendelevium 101	No nobelium 102	Lr lawrencium 103

Gold

The actinides are a group of 15 elements at the bottom of the periodic table that take their name from actinium. They include radium and plutonium and are all very radioactive.

What is the lightest element?
The lightest element is hydrogen. It has just one proton in its nucleus and has an atomic mass of just one. The heaviest is osmium, which is 10 times denser than lead.

How do batteries work?
Batteries create electric currents from the reaction between two chemicals, one forming a positive electrode and the other a negative. The reaction creates an excess of electrons on the negative electrode, producing a current. Chemicals used include zinc chloride, strong alkaline chemicals and lithium.

What is electrolysis?
Electrolysis is a chemical reaction caused when an electric current is passed through a solution – the electrolyte. The effect is to make positive ions (or cations) move to the negative terminals (the cathode) and negative ions (or anions) move to the positive terminal (the anode).

What is a mixture?
Mixtures are substances that contain several chemical elements or compounds mixed in together but not chemically joined. The chemicals intermingle but do not react with each other, and with the right technique can often be separated. An example of a mixture is milk.

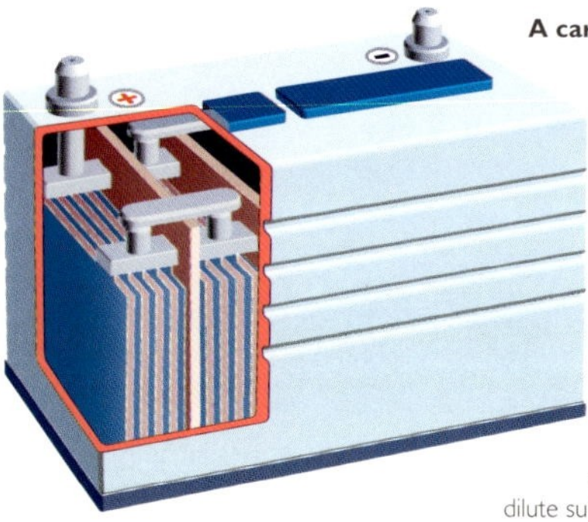

A car battery

In a lead-acid car battery, alternating plates of lead and lead oxide form negative and positive terminals, linked by a bath of dilute sulphuric acid – the electrolyte.

What is a chemical formula?
A chemical formula is a shorthand way of describing an atom, an ion or a molecule. Initial letters (sometimes plus an extra letter) usually identify the atom or ion; a little number indicates how many atoms are involved. The formula for water is H_2O, because each molecule consists of two hydrogen atoms and one oxygen atom.

What are compounds?

THEY ARE SUBSTANCES MADE FROM TWO OR MORE ELEMENTS JOINED TOGETHER. Every molecule in a compound is the same combination of atoms. Sodium chloride, for instance, is one atom of sodium joined to one of chlorine. Compounds have different properties to the elements that make them up. Sodium, for instance, spits when put in water; chlorine is a thick green gas. Yet sodium chloride is ordinary table salt!

What's the sea made of?
The sea is water with oxygen, carbon dioxide, nitrogen and various salts dissolved in it. The most abundant salt is common salt (sodium chloride). Others include Epsom salt (magnesium sulphate), magnesium chloride, potassium chloride, potassium bromide and potassium iodide.

What's the air made of?
Pure air is 78.9% nitrogen, 20.95% oxygen. There are traces of argon (0.93%), carbon dioxide (0.03%), helium (0.0005%), neon (0.018%), krypton (0.001%), xenon (0.0001%) and radon.

How do chemicals react?

WHEN SUBSTANCES REACT CHEMICALLY, THEIR ATOMS, IONS AND MOLECULES interact to form new combinations – separating elements from compounds or joining them together to form different compounds. Nearly all chemical reactions involve a change in energy – usually heat – as the bonds between particles are broken and formed.

Fire

Fire is a chemical reaction in which one substance gets so hot that it combines with oxygen in the air.

How do things dissolve?

When solids dissolve in liquid, it may look as if the solid disappears. Its atoms, ions or molecules are, in fact, still intact – but are separated and evenly dispersed throughout the liquid.

Why is nuclear power awesome?

THE ENERGY THAT BINDS TOGETHER AN ATOMIC NUCLEUS IS ENORMOUS, even though the nucleus itself is so small. In fact, as Einstein showed in 1905 with his theory of Special Relativity, the particles of the nucleus can also be regarded as pure energy. This enables nuclear power stations to generate huge amounts of power with just a few tonnes of nuclear fuel. It also gives nuclear bombs a massive and terrifying destructive power.

Nuclear fission

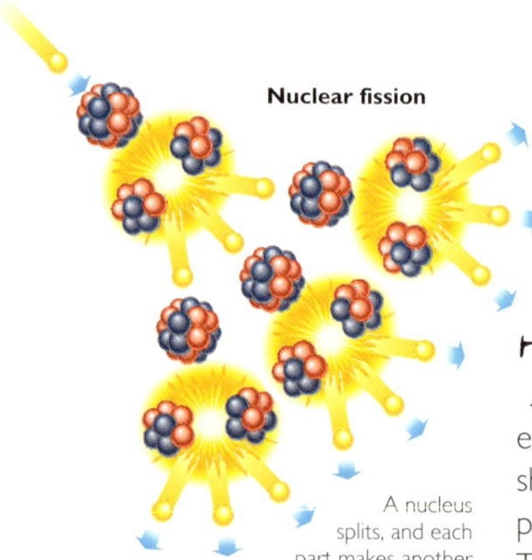

A nucleus splits, and each part makes another nucleus split, and so on, in a fission chain reaction.

What is nuclear fusion?

Nuclear energy is released by fusing or joining together small atoms like those of deuterium (a form of hydrogen). Nuclear fusion is the reaction that keeps stars glowing and provides energy for thermonuclear warheads. Scientists hope to find a way of harnessing nuclear fusion for power generation.

What is nuclear fission?

Nuclear fission releases nuclear energy by splitting big atomic nuclei – usually those of uranium. Neutrons are fired at the nuclei. As the neutrons smash into the nuclei they split off more neutrons, which bombard other nuclei, setting off a chain reaction.

What is an atomic bomb?

An atomic bomb or A-bomb is one of the two main kinds of nuclear weapon. An A-bomb relies on the explosive nuclear fission of uranium-235 or plutonium-239. Hydrogen bombs, also called H-bombs or thermonuclear weapons, rely on the fusion of hydrogen atoms to create explosions a thousand times more powerful.

How do nuclear power stations work?

Inside the reactor there are fuel rods made from pellets of uranium dioxide, separated by spacers. When the station goes 'on-line', a nuclear fission chain reaction is set up in the fuel rods. This is slowed down by control rods, which absorb the neutrons so that heat is produced steadily to drive the steam turbines that generate electricity.

A nuclear power station

A containment building houses the reactor vessel, keeping in heat, radioactivity and other energy.

Warmth from the nuclear reaction superheats water under very high pressure in the primary loop.

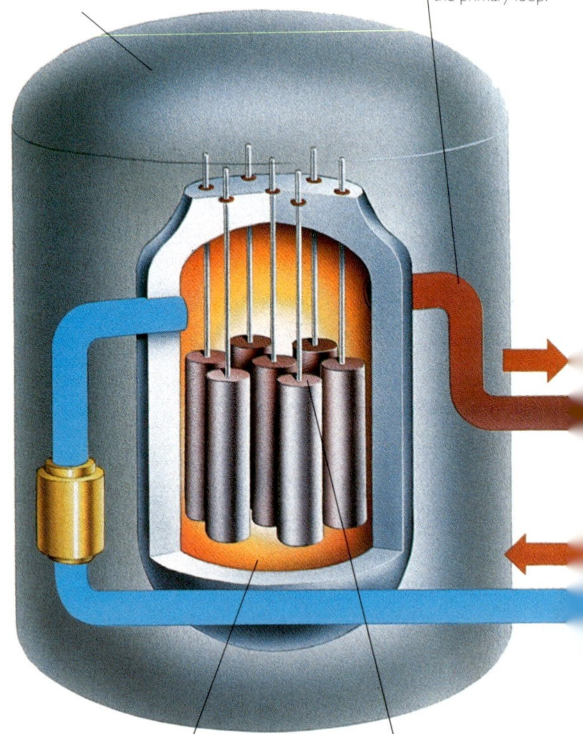

In the reactor vessel, nuclear fission releases tremendous amounts of heat energy.

The nuclear reactions take place in fuel rods in the reactor core.

What exactly is radioactivity?

THE ATOMS OF AN ELEMENT MAY COME IN SEVERAL DIFFERENT FORMS OR ISOTOPES. Each form has a different number of neutrons in the nucleus, indicated in the name, as in carbon-12 and carbon-14. The nuclei of some of these isotopes – the ones scientists call radioisotopes – are unstable, and they decay (break up), releasing radiation, consisting of streams of particles called alpha, beta and gamma rays. This is what radioactivity is.

What does radiation do to you?

It causes radiation sickness. With a very high dose, the victim dies in a few hours from nerve damage. With a less high dose, the victim dies after a week or so from damage to the gut or a complete collapse of the body's resistance to disease. Lower doses of radiation can cause cancer (including leukaemia) and defects in new-born babies.

How can radioactivity be used to indicate age?

Radioactivity proceeds at a very steady rate. So by measuring how much of a substance has decayed radioactively, you can tell how old it is. With once-living things, the best radioactive isotope to measure is carbon-14. This form of dating is called carbon dating.

Who invented the atomic bomb?

The first atomic bombs were developed in the USA towards the end of the Second World War by a brilliant team of scientists under the leadership of Robert Oppenheimer (1904–1967). His colleagues included Leo Szilard (1898–1964) and Otto Frisch (1904–1979). Together they created the first two A-bombs, which were dropped on Hiroshima and Nagasaki in Japan in 1945 with devastating effect.

What is half-life?

No-one can predict when an atomic nucleus will decay. But scientists can predict how long it will take for half the particles in a substance to decay. This is its half-life. Strontium-90 has a half-life of 9 minutes. Uranium-238 has a half-life of 4.5 billion years.

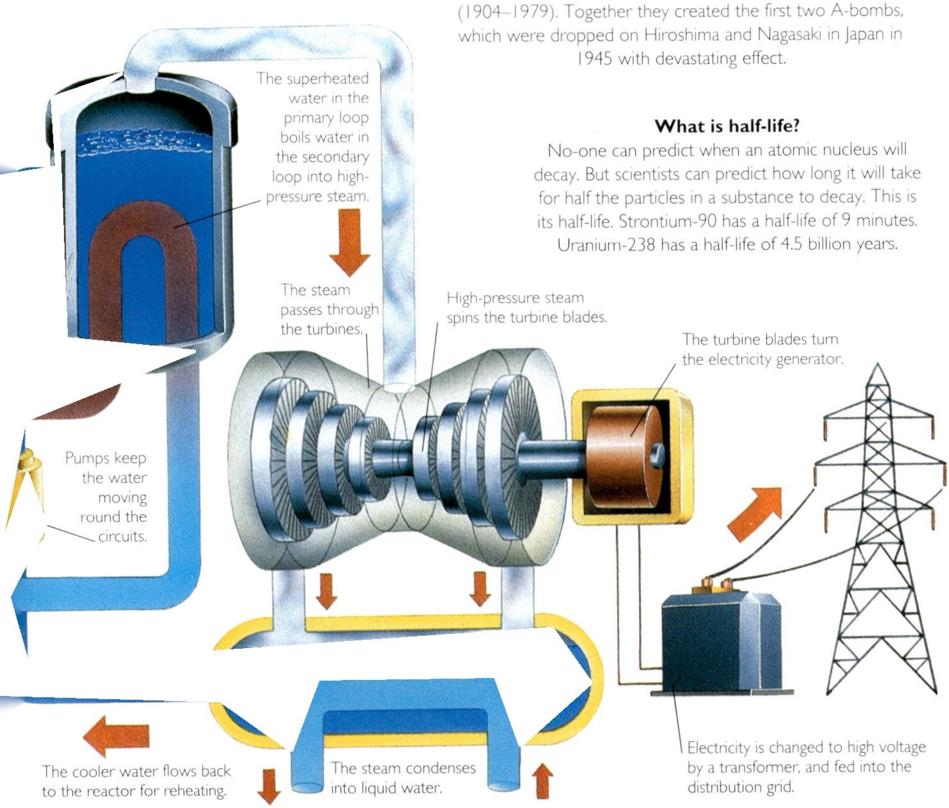

A buoy at sea

What's so special about water?

WATER IS SPECIAL IN MANY WAYS, AND IS ESSENTIAL TO ALL LIVING THINGS. Water is chemically neutral, yet dissolves many substances, which is why it is so important for life. It is denser as a liquid than a solid and so expands when it freezes. Water is found naturally in all of its three states of matter – solid ice, liquid water and gaseous water vapour. This is unusual, because of the strong bonds between its two hydrogen atoms and one oxygen atom. When cooled, most substances with similar sized atoms to water do not freeze until –30°C (–22°F). Water freezes at a much higher temperature, 0°C (32°F).

Why do things float?
When an object is immersed in water, the weight of the object pushes it down. But the water around it pushes it back up with a force equal to the weight of water displaced (pushed out of the way). The object sinks until its weight is equalled by the upthrust, then floats.

Hydroelectric dam

Hydroelectric power depends on the fact that water is drawn downwards by gravity to turn the turbine that generates electricity.

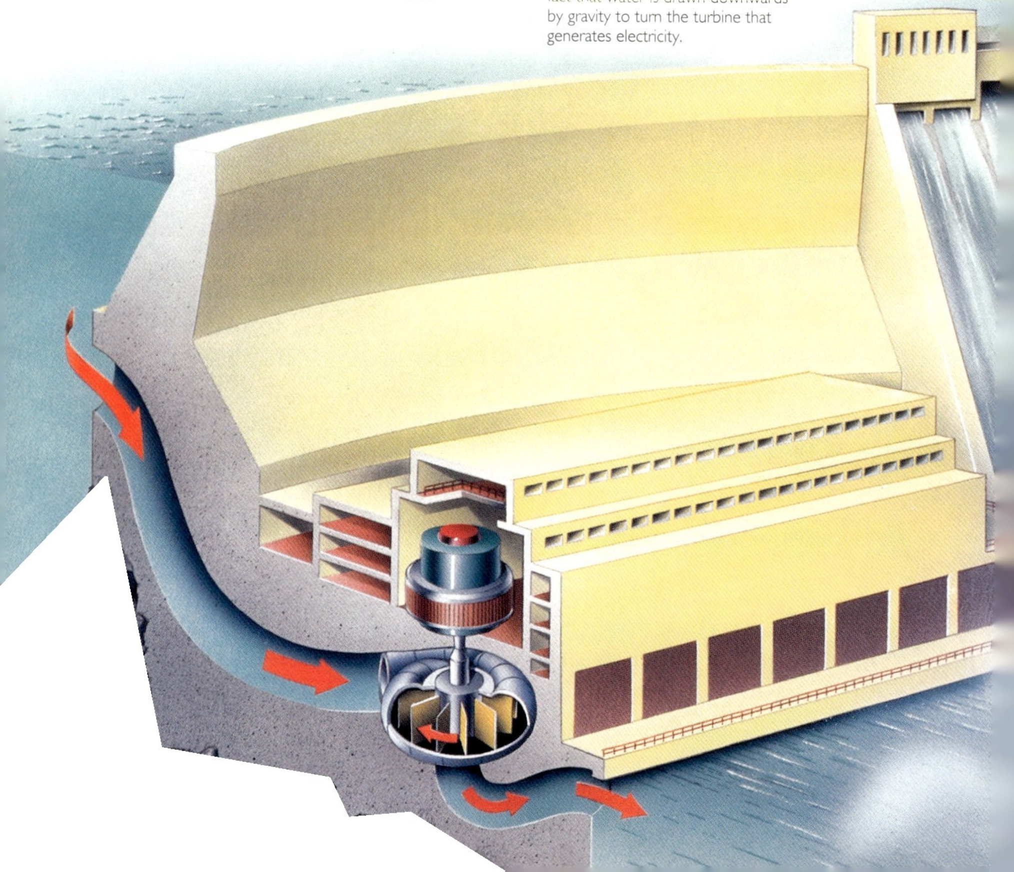

What is hydraulic power?

Fluids like water are incompressible – that is, they cannot be squashed. So if you push fluid through a pipe, it will push out the other end. Hydraulic power uses fluid-filled pipes working like this to drive things very smoothly. Hydraulic means water, but most hydraulic systems use oil to avoid rust problems.

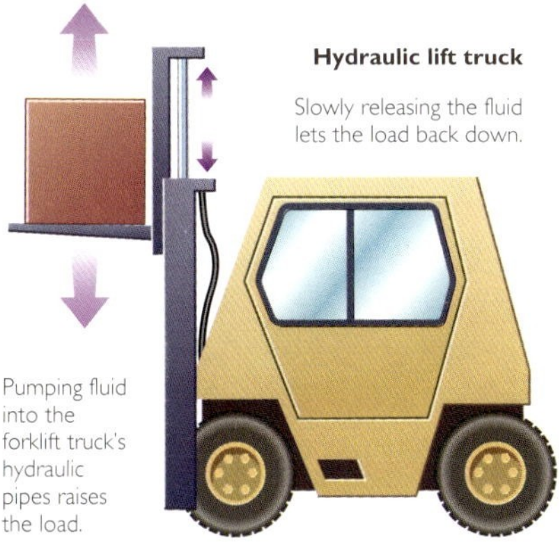

Hydraulic lift truck

Slowly releasing the fluid lets the load back down.

Pumping fluid into the forklift truck's hydraulic pipes raises the load.

What is heavy water?

Heavy water is deuterium oxide – water that is a little heavier than ordinary water because it contains the hydrogen isotope deuterium rather than ordinary hydrogen. Heavy water is used in the nuclear industry to slow down nuclear reactions.

How much water is there in the body?

Water is found in nearly every cell of the body, which is why human bodies are almost three-quarters water. Women's bodies have slightly less water than men's, and children's bodies slightly less than women.

Why do plants need water?

Plants contain an even higher proportion of water than the human body. Plants need water for building cells, and also for transporting nutrients from the roots to the leaves where they are needed.

Why does sweating keep you cool?

Because sweat is nearly all water, and water needs warmth to turn to vapour – which we call 'drying'. Watery sweat dries from the skin by taking warmth from the body. This makes the body cooler.

The bigger the head of water – that is, the deeper it is and the further it has to fall – the greater the hydroelectric power.

What is hydroelectric power?

Hydroelectric power or HEP is electricity generated by turbines turned by falling water. Typically, hydroelectric power stations are sited inside dams built to create a big fall or 'head' in the water.

Who made the first waterwheels?

Nobody knows for sure, but wheels turned by water to generate power were described by Ancient Greek writers over 2,000 years ago.

Why do icebergs float in the sea?

WHEN MOST THINGS GET COLDER, THEY CONTRACT, AND WHEN MOST LIQUIDS freeze they get very much smaller. Water is unique in that it contracts only down to a certain temperature, 4°C (39.2°F). If it gets colder still, it begins to expand, because the special bonds between the hydrogen atoms in the water begin to break down. When it freezes, water expands so much that ice is actually lighter (less dense) than water, so ice floats. But it is only a little lighter, so icebergs float with almost nine-tenths below the water line – which is why they are so dangerous to ships.

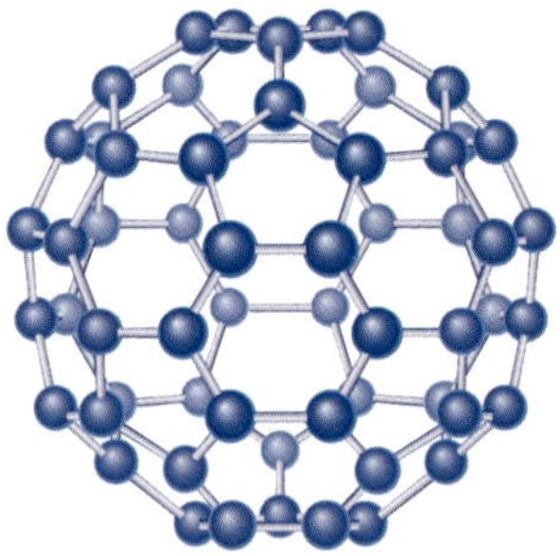

Carbon buckyball

This is one molecule of buckminster fullerene made from dozens of carbon atoms linked together in a ball.

What are buckyballs?

Before 1990, carbon was known in two main forms or allotropes – diamond and graphite. In 1990, a third allotrope was created. Its molecule looks like a football or the domed stadium roofs created by American architect Buckminster Fuller. And so this allotrope is called, after him, a buckyball.

Who discovered the shape of DNA?

The discovery in 1953 that every molecule of DNA is shaped like a twisted rope ladder or 'double helix' was one of the great scientific breakthroughs of the 20th century. Maurice Wilkins and Rosalind Franklin did the groundwork for the discovery. Francis Crick and James Watson, two young researchers at Cambridge University, UK, had the inspiration and won the Nobel Prize.

What is a polymer?

Polymers are substances made from long chains of thousands of small carbon-based molecules, called monomers, strung together. Some polymers occur naturally, such as wool and cotton, but plastics such as nylon and polythene are man-made polymers.

How is oil refined?

Oil drilled from the ground, called crude oil, is separated into different substances, mainly by distillation. This means the crude oil is heated until it evaporates. The substances are then drawn off and condensed from the vapour at different temperatures. The molecules of heavier oils may then be 'cracked' by heating under pressure.

What is DNA?

DNA IS DEOXYRIBONUCLEIC ACID. THIS IS THE AMAZING LONG DOUBLE-SPIRAL molecule that is found inside every living cell. It is made up of long chains of sugars and phosphates linked by pairs of chemical 'bases'– adenine, cytosine, guanine and thymine. The order in which these bases recur provides in code form the instructions for all the cell's activities, and for the lifeplan of the entire organism.

DNA molecule

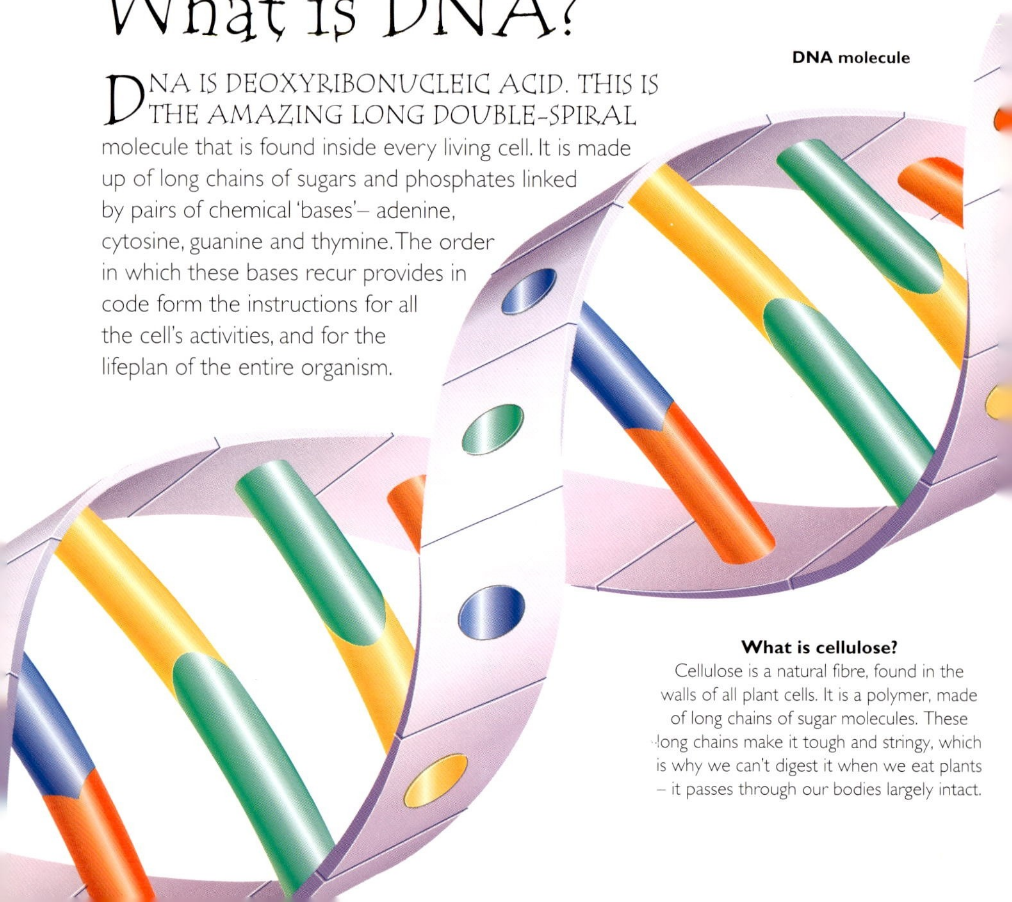

What is cellulose?

Cellulose is a natural fibre, found in the walls of all plant cells. It is a polymer, made of long chains of sugar molecules. These long chains make it tough and stringy, which is why we can't digest it when we eat plants – it passes through our bodies largely intact.

How is natural oil made?
Oil is formed from tiny plants and animals that lived in warm seas millions of years ago. As they died, they were slowly buried beneath the sea-bed. As the sea-bed sediments hardened into rock, the remains of the organisms were turned to oil and squeezed into cavities in the rock.

What is oil?
Oils are thick liquids that won't mix with water. Mineral oils used for motor fuel are hydrocarbons – that is, complex organic chemicals made from hydrogen and carbon.

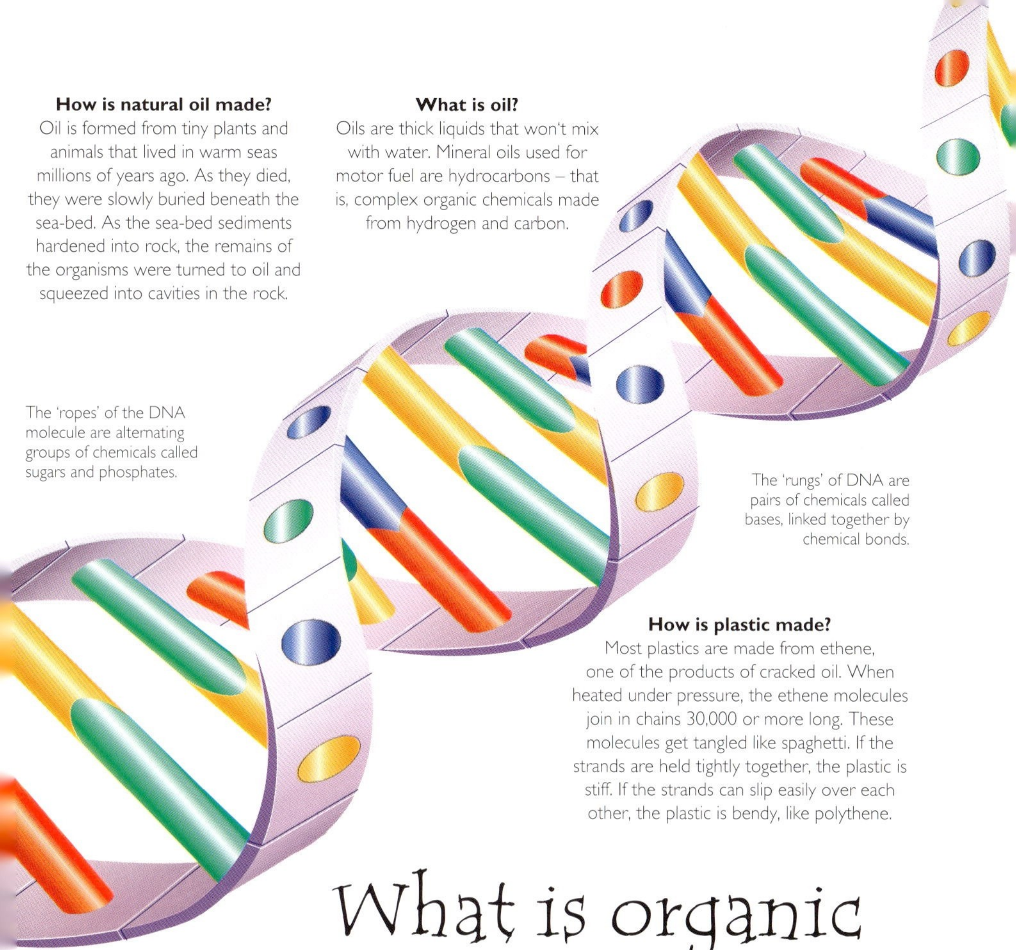

The 'ropes' of the DNA molecule are alternating groups of chemicals called sugars and phosphates.

The 'rungs' of DNA are pairs of chemicals called bases, linked together by chemical bonds.

How is plastic made?
Most plastics are made from ethene, one of the products of cracked oil. When heated under pressure, the ethene molecules join in chains 30,000 or more long. These molecules get tangled like spaghetti. If the strands are held tightly together, the plastic is stiff. If the strands can slip easily over each other, the plastic is bendy, like polythene.

What is organic chemistry?

ORGANIC CHEMISTRY IS THE CHEMISTRY OF CARBON AND ITS COMPOUNDS. Carbon's unique atomic structure means it links atoms together in long chains, rings or other shapes to form thousands of different compounds. These include complex molecules – such as DNA – that are the basis of life, which is why carbon chemistry is called organic chemistry.

What is a carbon chain?
Carbon atoms often link together like the links of a chain to form very long thin molecules – as in the molecule of propane, which consists of three carbon atoms in a row, with hydrogen atoms attached.

What are aromatics?
Benzene is a clear liquid organic chemical found in coal tar. It can be harmful, but has many uses, for example as a cleaning fluid and in manufacturing dyes. It has distinctive hexagonal molecules made of six carbon atoms and six hydrogen atoms and called a benzene ring. It also has a distinctive aroma, which is why chemicals that have a benzene ring are called aromatics.

What is the carbon cycle?
Carbon circulates like this: animals breathe out carbon as carbon dioxide. Plants take in carbon dioxide from the air, convert it into carbohydrates – and when animals eat plants, they take in carbon again.

What are carbohydrates?
Carbohydrates are chemicals made only of carbon, hydrogen and oxygen atoms – including sugars, starches and cellulose. Most animals rely on carbohydrate sugars such as glucose and sucrose for energy.

The knock-on effect

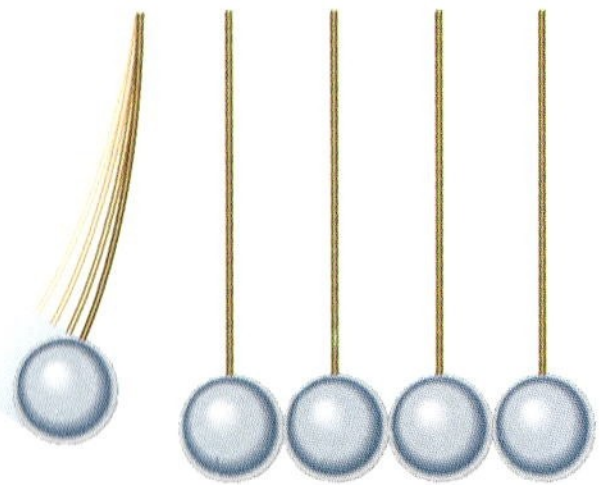

In this toy, each swinging ball knocks into the next, passing momentum along.

What is a knock-on effect?

When two objects collide, their combined momentum remains the same, if nothing else interferes. So if one object loses momentum, this momentum must be passed on to the other object, making it move. This is essentially a knock-on effect.

What is a turning force?

When something fixed in one place, called a fulcrum, is pushed or pulled elsewhere, it turns around the fulcrum. When you push a door shut, that push is the turning force, and the hinge is the fulcrum.

When your toboggan hits a rock, your hat carries on without you. Its momentum throws it forwards.

What was Newton's breakthrough?

Sir Isaac Newton's breakthrough, in 1665, was to realize that all movement in the Universe is governed by three simple rules, which we now called Newton's Laws of Motion. The First is about inertia and momentum. For his three Laws of Motion, read on.

What's the difference between inertia and momentum?

Inertia is the tendency of things to stay still unless they are forced to move. Momentum is the tendency for things to keep going once they are moving, unless forced to stop or slow. This is the First Law of Motion.

What is acceleration?

Acceleration is how fast something gains speed. The larger the force and the lighter the object, the greater the acceleration. This is Newton's Second law of Motion.

What happens with every action?

This is Newton's Third Law of Motion – for every action, there is an equal and opposite reaction. Which means that whenever something moves, there is a balance of forces pushing in opposite directions. When you push your legs against water to swim, for instance, the water pushes back on your legs equally hard.

How do things get moving?

THINGS ONLY MOVE IF FORCED TO MOVE. SO WHEN SOMETHING STARTS MOVING, there must be a force involved – whether it is visible, like someone pushing, or gravity, which makes things fall. But once they are moving, things will carry on moving at the same speed and in the same direction, until another force is applied – typically friction.

Why do things go round?

IF ONLY ONE FORCE IS INVOLVED, THINGS WILL ALWAYS MOVE IN A STRAIGHT LINE. This is called linear motion. Things go round when there is more than one force involved. A ball loops through the air because gravity is pulling it down while its momentum is pushing it on – less and less strongly. A wheel goes round on its axle because there is one force trying to make it carry on in a straight line and another keeping it the same distance from the axle.

What is uniform motion?
Uniform motion is when an object carries on travelling at exactly the same speed in exactly the same direction.

A toboggan ride, courtesy of the force of gravity

Once gravity has overcome your toboggan's inertia and got you swishing downhill, its momentum will keep it going until something stops it.

What's the difference between velocity and speed?
Speed is how fast something is going. Velocity is how fast something is going and in which direction. Speed is therefore called a scalar quantity; velocity a vector.

What is Special Relativity?
The theory of Special Relativity shows how both space and time can be measured only relatively – that is, in comparison to something else. This means that time can speed up or slow down, depending on how fast you are moving.

Who was Einstein?
Albert Einstein (1897–1955) was the scientific genius who transformed science with his two big theories – Special Relativity (1905) and General Relativity (1915). The theory of Special Relativity was developed while he was working in the Swiss Patent Office in Bern.

What's the fastest thing in the Universe?
Light, which travels at 300,000 km (186,000 miles) per second. This is the one speed in the universe that is constant – that is, it always the same no matter how fast you are going when you measure it.

What is a force?

A FORCE IS WHAT MAKES SOMETHING MOVE – BY PUSHING IT OR PULLING IT in a particular direction. It may be an invisible force, like gravity, or a visible force like a kick, but it always causes something to either accelerate or decelerate or change shape. Forces always work in pairs – whenever a force pushes, it must push against something else equally – which is why guns kick back violently when fired.

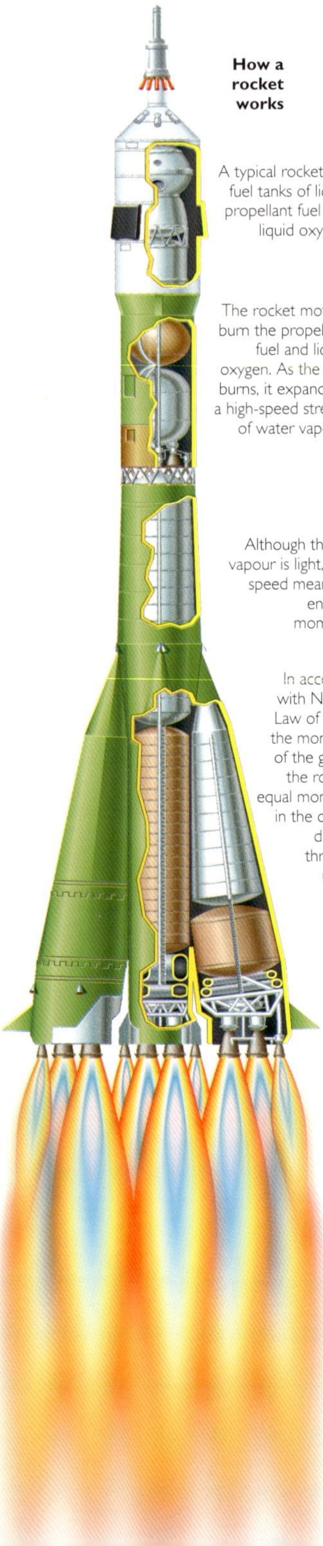

How a rocket works

A typical rocket has fuel tanks of liquid propellant fuel and liquid oxygen.

The rocket motors burn the propellant fuel and liquid oxygen. As the fuel burns, it expands in a high-speed stream of water vapour.

Although the water vapour is light, its high speed means it has enormous momentum.

In accordance with Newton's Law of Motion, the momentum of the gas gives the rocket an equal momentum in the opposite direction, thrusting it upward.

What's the difference between mass and weight?

Mass is the amount of matter in an object. It is the same wherever you measure it, even on the Moon. Weight is a measure of the force of gravity on an object. It varies according to where you measure it.

What is power?

Power is the rate at which work is done – a high-powered engine is an engine that can move a great deal of weight very quickly. Power is also the rate at which energy is transferred – a large amount of electric power might be needed to heat a large quantity of water.

What is gravity?

Gravity is the invisible force of attraction between every bit of matter in the Universe. Its strength depends on the mass of the objects involved and their distance apart.

What did Galileo do on the Tower of Pisa?

The Italian scientist and astronomer Galileo Galilei (1564–1642) is said to have dropped metal balls of different weights from the Leaning Tower of Pisa to show that they all fall at the same speed.

What did a great scientist learn from an apple?

The mathematician and physicist Sir Isaac Newton is said to have developed his ideas about gravity while sitting one day under an apple tree. As he watched an apple fall to the ground, it occurred to him in a flash that the apple was not merely falling but was being pulled towards the ground by an invisible force. This is the force he called gravity.

How is force measured?

Force is measured in newtons, in honour of Sir Isaac Newton. A newton is the force needed to accelerate 1 kilogram by 1 metre per second every second.

What is friction?

Friction is the force between two things rubbing together, which may be brake pads on a bicycle wheel or air molecules against an aeroplane. Friction tends to slow things down, making them hot as their momentum is converted into heat.

How fast does a stone fall?

At first, the stone falls faster and faster at a rate of 9.8 metres (32 ft) per second at every second. But as the stone's speed accelerates, air resistance increases until it becomes so great that the stone cannot fall any faster. It now continues to fall at the same velocity, called the terminal velocity.

How does gravity hold you down?

THE MUTUAL GRAVITATIONAL ATTRACTION BETWEEN THE MASS of your body and the mass of the Earth pulls them together. If you jump off a wall, the Earth pulls you towards the ground. You also pull the Earth towards you, but because you are tiny while the Earth is huge, you move a lot and the Earth barely moves at all.

Why can you jump higher on the Moon?

The Moon is much smaller than the Earth, so its gravity is much weaker. Astronauts weigh six times less on the Moon than they do on Earth – and can jump much higher!

Does gravity vary?

An object's gravitational pull varies with its mass and its distance. In fact, gravity diminishes precisely in proportion to its distance away, squared. You can work out the force of gravity between two objects by multiplying their masses and dividing by the square of the distance between them. This sum works all over the Universe with pinpoint accuracy.

Why do satellites go round the Earth?

Satellites are whizzing through space at exactly the right height for their speed. The Earth's gravity tries to pull them down to Earth, but they are travelling so fast that they go on zooming round the Earth just as fast as the Earth pulls them in.

Orbiting the Earth

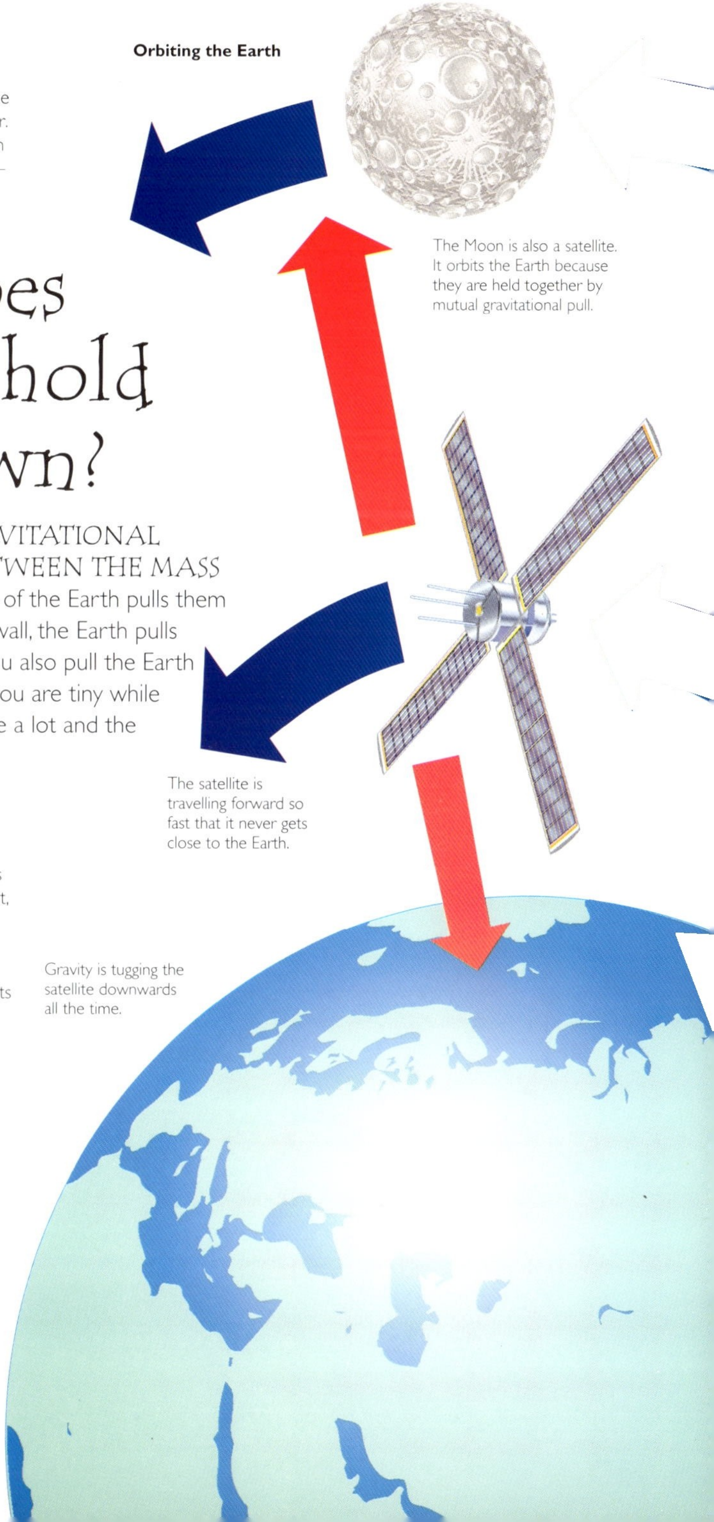

The Moon is also a satellite. It orbits the Earth because they are held together by mutual gravitational pull.

The satellite is travelling forward so fast that it never gets close to the Earth.

Gravity is tugging the satellite downwards all the time.

How is energy conserved?
Energy can be neither created nor destroyed. When energy is converted from one form to another, there is always exactly the same amount of energy afterwards as there was before. In this way energy is conserved, even when converted into a different form.

What is energy efficiency?
Some machines waste a great deal of energy, while others waste very little. The energy efficiency of a machine is measured by the proportion of energy it wastes. Waste energy is usually lost as heat.

How are energy and mass linked?
Energy is a form of mass; mass is a form of energy. In nuclear reactions, tiny amounts of mass are changed into huge quantities of energy.

What's absolute zero?
Absolute zero is the coldest possible temperature, the temperature at which atoms stop moving altogether. This happens at –273.15°C (–459.67°F), or 0 on the Kelvin scale.

What is conduction?
Conduction is one of the three ways in which heat moves. It involves heat spreading from hot areas to cold areas as moving particles knock into one another. The other ways are convection, in which warm air or water rises, and radiation, which is rays of invisible infrared light.

How fossil fuels were formed

Millions of years ago, plants absorbed the Sun's energy and converted it into new fibres as they grew.

The stored energy in the plant fibres was concentrated into coal as the fibres were buried and squeezed beneath layers of sediment over millions of years.

What is energy?

ENERGY TAKES MANY FORMS. HEAT ENERGY BOILS WATER, KEEPS US WARM and drives engines. Chemical energy fuels cars and aeroplanes. Electrical energy drives many small machines and keeps lights glowing. Almost every form of energy can be converted into other forms. But whatever form it is in, energy is essentially the capacity for making something happen or, as scientists put it, 'doing work'.

Where does our energy come from?

NEARLY ALL OF OUR ENERGY COMES TO US ULTIMATELY FROM THE SUN. Some we get directly via solar power cells. Most comes indirectly via fossil fuels (coal and oil), which got their energy from the fossilized plants (and other organisms) of which they are made. The plants got their energy directly from the sun by a process called photosynthesis.

400 million°C (720 million°F) is the highest temperature ever measured – in a nuclear fusion experiment in USA.

The highest air temperature ever recorded is 58°C (136°F) in Libya.

Earth's lowest air temperature ever measured is –88°C (–190°F) in Antarctica.

The lowest temperature ever measured is almost –273.15°C (–459.67°F) in a Finnish laboratory.

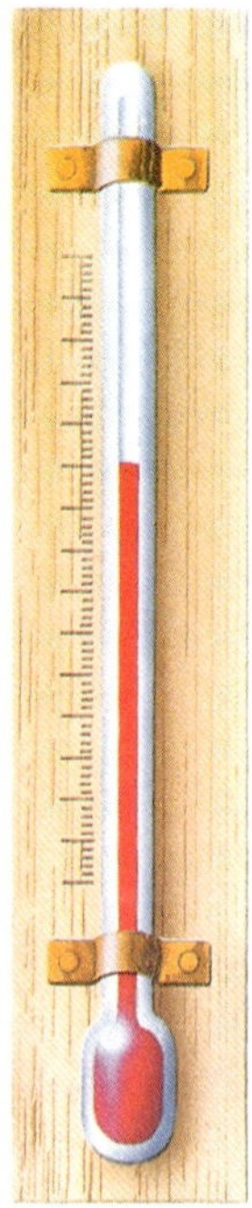

Spirit thermometer for measuring normal air temperatures

What's the difference between heat and temperature?
Heat is molecules moving. It is a form of energy – the combined energy of all the moving molecules. Temperature, on the other hand, is simply a measure of how fast all the molecules are moving.

How do you convert Fahrenheit to Celsius?
You can convert from Fahrenheit to Celsius by subtracting 32 then dividing by nine and multiplying by five. You can convert from Celsius to Fahrenheit by dividing by five, multiplying by nine and adding 32.

How is temperature measured?
Temperature is usually measured with a thermometer. Some thermometers have a metal strip that bends according to how hot it is. But most contain a liquid, such as mercury, in a tube. As it gets warmer, the liquid expands, and its level rises in the tube. The level of the liquid indicates the temperature.

The deepest coal (called anthracite) is squashed to almost pure black carbon, and provides a very concentrated form of energy.

Fuel buried less deep is less squashed. This less concentrated fuel is called brown coal or lignite.

Refraction

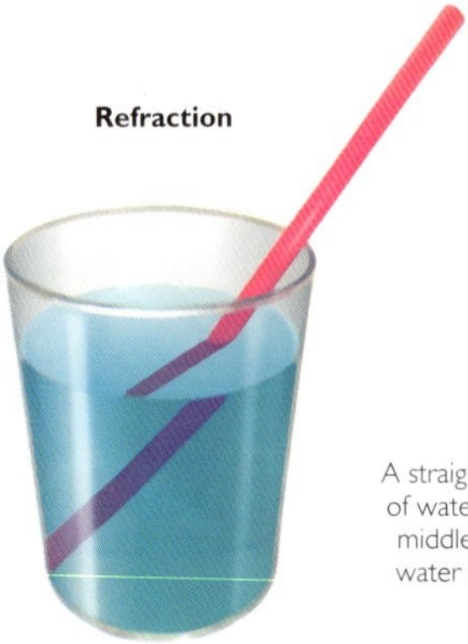

A straight rod dipped in a glass of water seems to bend in the middle, because the glass and water refract (bend) the light.

How is light bent?
Light rays are bent when they are refracted. This happens when they strike a transparent material like glass or water, at an angle. The different materials slow the light waves down so that they slew round, like car wheels driving on to sand.

How do fibre optic cables bend light?
Actually they don't bend light, but reflect it round corners. Inside a cable are lots of bundles of glass fibres. Light rays zig-zag along the inside of each fibre, reflecting first one side, then the other. In this way, light can be transmitted through the cable no matter what route it takes.

Why is the sun red?
The sun is only red at sunrise and sunset, when the sun is low in the sky and sunlight reaches us only after passing a long way through the dense lower layers of the atmosphere. Particles in the air absorb shorter, bluer wavelengths of light or reflect them away from us, leaving just the red.

How do your eyes see things?

LIGHT SOURCES SUCH AS THE SUN, STARS AND ELECTRIC LIGHT SHINE light rays straight into your eyes. Everything else you see only by reflected light – that is, by light rays that bounce off things. So you can see things only if there is a light source throwing light on to them. Otherwise, they look black, and you can't see them at all.

How do mirrors work?
Most mirrors are made of ordinary glass, but the back is silvered – coated with a shiny metal that perfectly reflects all the light that hits it – at exactly the same angle.

Does light travel in waves?
In the last century, most scientists believed light did travel in tiny waves rather than bullet-like particles. Now they agree it can be both, and it is probably best to think of light as vibrating packets of energy.

What are photons?
Photons are almost infinitesimally small particles of light. They have no mass and there are billions of them in a single beam of light.

Reflection

You can see an object such as a plant in a pot by the light reflected from it.

How do things absorb light?
When light rays hit a surface, some bounce off, but others are absorbed by atoms in the surface, warming it up very slightly. Each kind of atom absorbs particular wavelengths (colours) of light. The colour of the surface depends on which wavelengths of light are absorbed and which reflected. You see a leaf as green because the leaf has soaked up all colours but green, and you see only the reflected green light.

What happens at an interference fringe?

INTERFERENCE IS WHAT HAPPENS WHEN TWO LIGHT WAVES MEET EACH OTHER. If the waves are in step with each other, they reinforce each other. This is positive interference, and you see bright light. If they are out of step, they may cancel each other out. This is negative interference, and you see shadow. Interference fringes are bands of light and shade created by alternating positive and negative interference.

The image in a mirror is back-to-front or reversed. Left is on the right, and right is on the left – a mirror image! A photograph gives a true right-way-round image.

The reflection of the plant forms an image that appears to be behind the mirror – as if you were looking at it through a window.

Why is the sky blue?
Sunlight is white – which means it contains all the colours of the rainbow. The sky is blue because air molecules scatter – reflect in all directions – more blue from sunlight towards our eyes than other colours.

What is an incident ray?
When scientists talk about reflections, they distinguish between the light falling on the reflector (which may be a mirror) and the light reflected. Incident rays are the rays hitting the reflector.

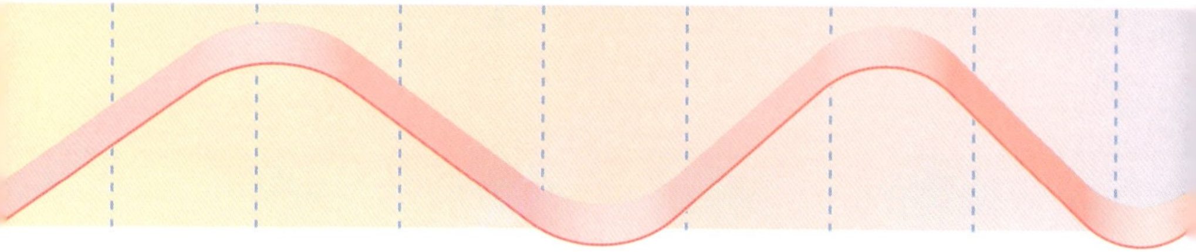

All the different colours of light have different wavelengths. The longest waves we can see are red.

What is the electromagnetic spectrum?

LIGHT IS JUST A SMALL PART OF THE WIDE RANGE OF RADIATION EMITTED BY ATOMS – the only part we can see. This range of radiation is called the electromagnetic spectrum and ranges from long waves – such as radio waves and microwaves – to short waves – such as X-rays and gamma rays.

Why can't you see ultraviolet?
Ultraviolet light is light with wavelengths too short for the human eye to register.

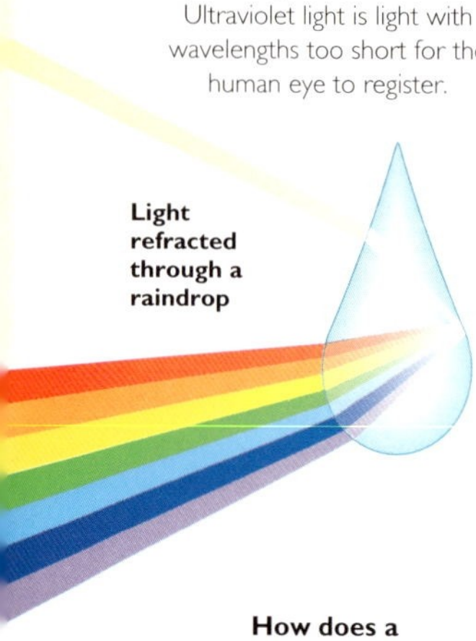

Light refracted through a raindrop

How does a prism split colours?
Prisms split white light into separate colours by refracting (bending) it. The longer the wavelength of the light, the more it is refracted. So long wavelength colours emerge from the prism at a different point from short wavelength colours.

What is infrared?
Infrared is light with wavelengths too long for the human eye to register. But you can often feel infrared light as warmth.

How do TV signals travel?
TV signals travel in one of three ways. Terrestrial broadcasts are beamed out from transmitters as radio waves to be picked up by TV aerials. Satellite broadcasts are sent up to satellites as microwaves, then picked up by satellite dishes. Cable broadcasts travel as electrical or light signals along underground cables, straight to the TV set.

How do X-rays see through you?
X-rays are stopped only by the bones and especially dense bits of the body. They pass through the soft bits to hit a photographic plate on the far side of the body, where they leave a silhouette of the skeleton.

How do CT scans work?
CT (computed tomography) scans run X-ray beams right round the body, and pick up how much is absorbed with special sensors. A computer analyses the data to create a complete 'slice' through the body.

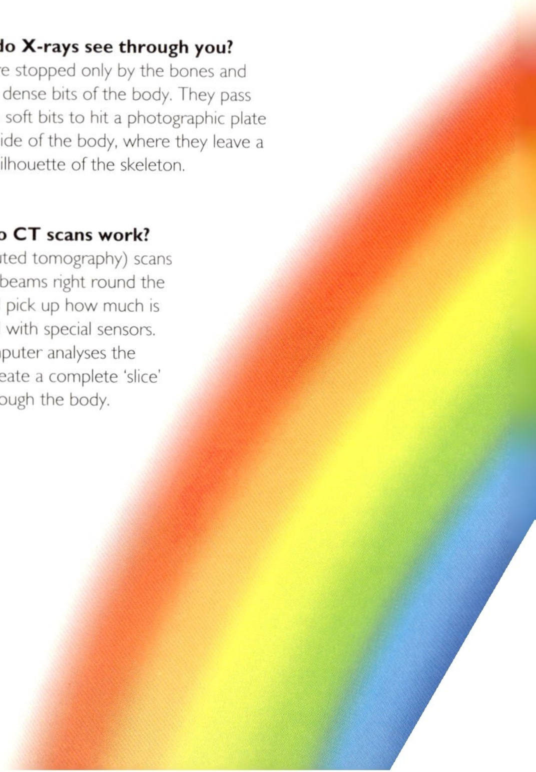

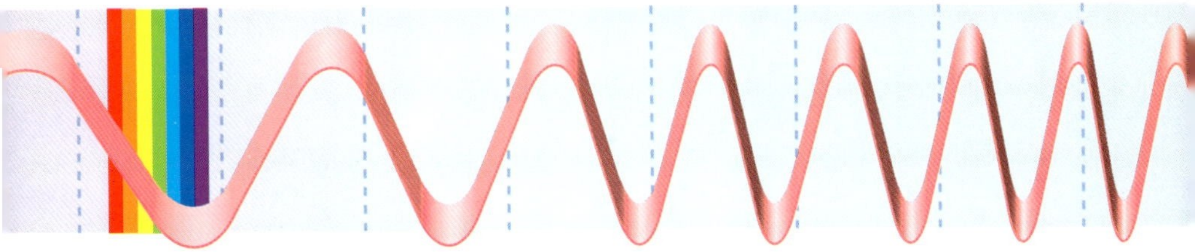

The shortest waves of light we can see are violet.

Electromagnetic spectrum

Who made the first radio broadcast?

Italian inventor Guglielmo Marconi first sent radio signals over 1.6 km (1 mile) in 1895. In 1898, he sent a message in Morse code across the English Channel. In 1901, he sent a radio message across the Atlantic.

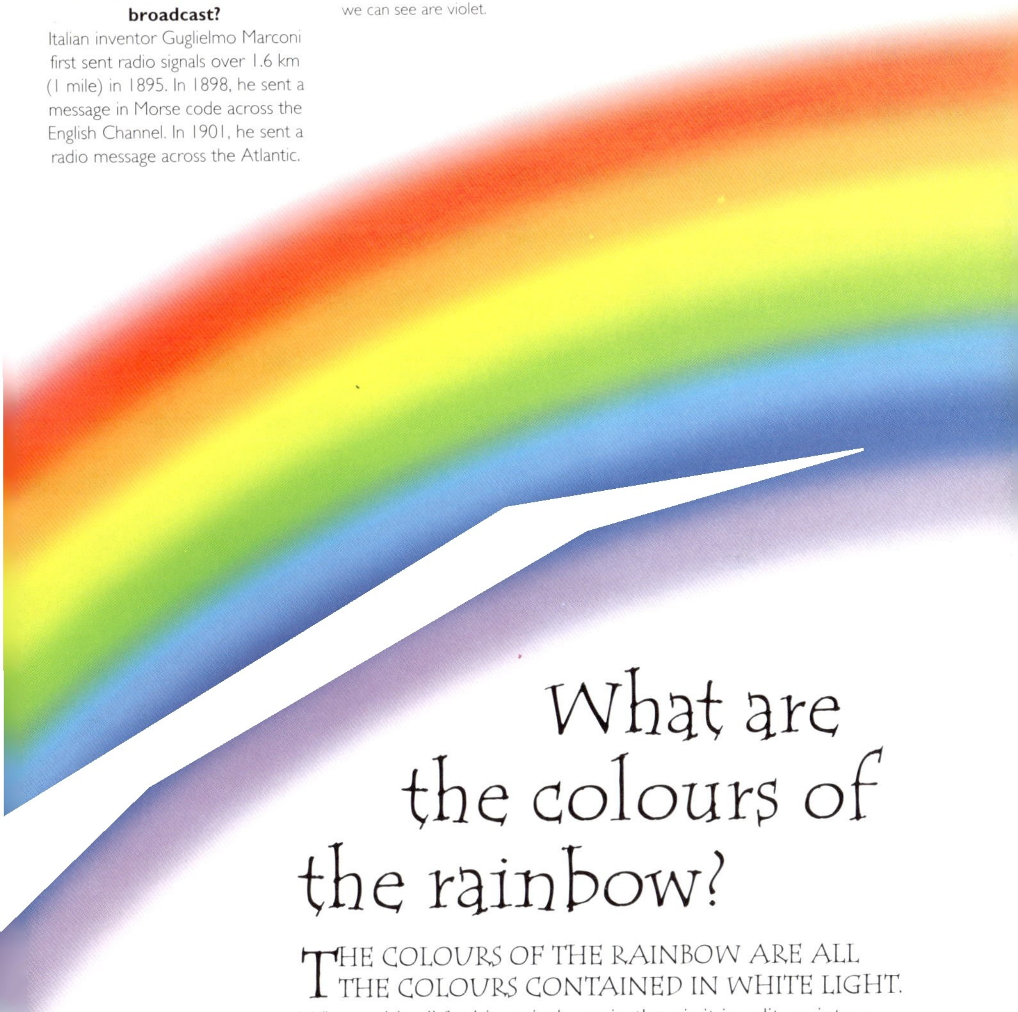

What are the colours of the rainbow?

THE COLOURS OF THE RAINBOW ARE ALL THE COLOURS CONTAINED IN WHITE LIGHT. When white light hits raindrops in the air, it is split up into a rainbow of colours, because each colour of light is refracted by the rainbow to a different extent. The colours of the rainbow appear in this order: red, orange, yellow, green, blue, indigo, violet.

Rainbows are formed by the reflection of the Sun off billions of drops of moisture in the air.

What is an electric current?
A current is a continuous stream of electrical charge. It happens only when there is a complete, unbroken 'circuit' for the current to flow through – typically a loop of copper wire.

What is a silicon chip?
A silicon chip is an electronic circuit implanted in a small crystal of semi-conducting silicon, in such a way that it can be manufactured in huge numbers. This was the predecessor to the microprocessors that make computers work.

How do electric currents flow?
The charge in an electric current is electrons that have broken free from their atoms. None of them moves very far, but the current is passed on as they bang into each other like rows of marbles.

Lightning flashes from a thundercloud when a massive negative electrical charge builds up in the base of the cloud.

Silicon chip

Complex electrical circuits can be printed on to a tiny silicon chip.

Why does your hair go frizzy?

WHEN YOU COMB DRY HAIR, TINY ELECTRONS ARE KNOCKED OFF the atoms in the comb as it rubs past. Your hair is coated with these tiny negative electrical charges and so is attracted to anything that has its normal quota of electrons, or more. An electric charge made like this is called 'static' because it does not move. Try rubbing a balloon on your jumper to create a static charge, then you can stick it on the wall.

What are the best conductors?
The best conductors are metals like copper and silver. Water is also a good conductor. Superconductors are materials like aluminium, which is cooled until it transmits electricity almost without resistance.

Lightning flashes to the ground to discharge because it always carries a slight positive electrical charge.

What makes lightning flash?

LIGHTNING FLASHES PRODUCE 100 MILLION VOLTS OF STATIC ELECTRICITY.

Lightning is created when raindrops and ice crystals inside a thundercloud become electrically charged as they are flung together, losing or gaining electrons from each other. Negatively charged particles build up at the base of the cloud. When this charge has built up enough, it discharges as lightning, either flashing within the cloud or forking between the cloud and the ground.

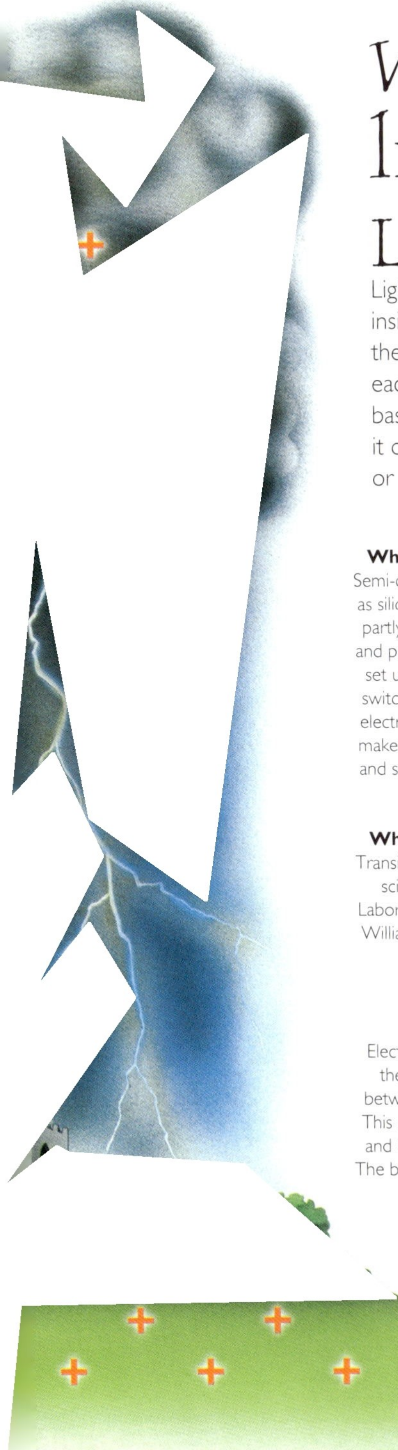

What is a semi-conductor?

Semi-conductors are materials such as silicon or germanium, which are partly resistant to electric current and partly conducting. They can be set up so that the conductivity is switched on or off, creating a tiny electrical switch. They are used to make diodes, transistors and chips, and so are essential to electronics.

What is resistance?

Not all substances conduct electric currents equally well. Resistance is a substance's ability to block a flow of electric current.

Light bulb

The pressure of the electric current through the bulb's thin wire filament makes it glow.

Who invented transistors?

Transistors were invented by three scientists working at the Bell Laboratories in the USA in 1948 – William Shockley, Walter Brattain and John Bardeen.

What is a volt?

Electrical current flows as long as there is a difference in charge between two points in the circuit. This difference is called a potential and is measured in terms of volts. The bigger the difference, the bigger the voltage.

What is an alternating current?

A direct current (DC) flows in one direction only. Most hand-held torches use DC. Electricity in the house is alternating current (AC), which means it continually swaps direction as the generator's coil spins around past its electrodes.

How does electric light work?

An electric bulb has a very thin filament of tungsten wire inside a glass bulb filled with argon or nitrogen gas. When current flows through such a thin wire, the resistance is so great that the wire heats up and glows brightly. If it wasn't surrounded by non-reactive nitrogen or argon gas, it would quickly burn through.

What is a magnetic pole?

MAGNETISM IS THE INVISIBLE FORCE THAT DRAWS TOGETHER SOME METALS, such as iron and steel – or pushes them apart. This force is especially strong at each end of the magnet. These two powerful ends are called poles. One is called the north (or north-seeking) pole, because if the magnet is suspended freely this pole swings round until it points north. The other is called the south pole. If the opposite poles of two magnets meet, they will be drawn together. If the same poles meet, the magnets will push each other apart.

Steel horseshoe magnet

When the paperclips come within the magnet's magnetic field, they become magnetized too, and so attract other paperclips.

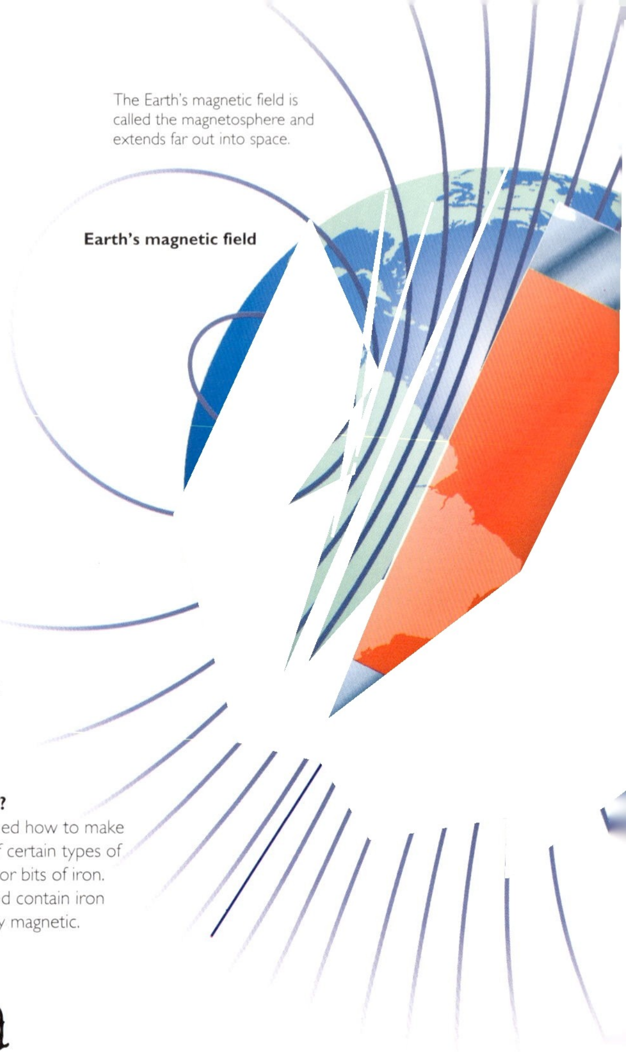

Earth's magnetic field

The Earth's magnetic field is called the magnetosphere and extends far out into space.

What is a magnetic field?

The magnetic field is the area around the magnet in which its effects are felt. It gets gradually weaker further away from the magnet. The Earth's magnetic field extends some 80,000 km (50,000 miles) out into space.

What is a lodestone?

Thousands of years before people learned how to make steel magnets, they found that lumps of certain types of rock can attract or repel each other, or bits of iron. These rocks are called lodestones, and contain iron oxide, which makes them naturally magnetic.

Why is the Earth like a magnet?

As the Earth spins, the swirling of its iron core turns the core into a giant magnet. It is a little like the way a bicycle dynamo generates an electric current. Like smaller magnets, the Earth's magnet has two poles, a north and a south. It is because Earth is a magnet that small magnets always point in the same direction if allowed to swivel freely.

How does sound travel?

EVERY SOUND IS CREATED BY VIBRATION, BE IT AN ELASTIC BAND TWANGING or a loudspeaker cone shaking to and fro. But you can't hear any sounds in a vacuum. This is because the sound reaches your ears as a vibration – and there must be something to vibrate. Normally, this is the air. When a sound source vibrates to and fro, it pushes the air around it to and fro. The sound travels through the air as it is pushed to and fro in a knock-on effect – that is by being alternately stretched and squeezed. This moving stretch and squeeze of air is called a sound wave.

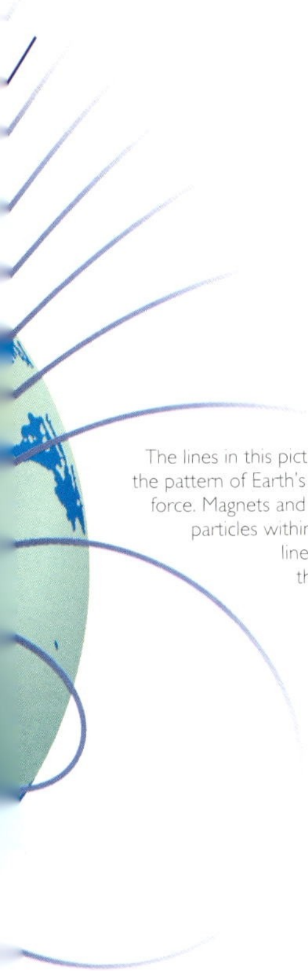

The lines in this picture show the pattern of Earth's magnetic force. Magnets and magnetic particles within the field line up along these lines.

What is resonance?

If allowed to vibrate freely, every object always tends to vibrate at the same rate. This is its natural frequency. You can make things vibrate faster or slower than this by jogging them at particular intervals. But if you can jog it at just the same rate as its natural frequency, it vibrates in sympathy and the vibrations become much stronger. This is resonance.

What is sound frequency?

Some sounds, like a car's squealing brakes, are very high-pitched. Others, like a booming bass drum, are very low-pitched. What makes them different is the frequency of the sound waves. If the sound waves follow very rapidly one after another, they are high-frequency and make a high sound. If there are long gaps between each wave, they are low-frequency and make a low sound. A low-frequency sound is about 20 Hz or waves per second. A high-frequency sound is 20,000 Hz or waves per second.

What is an echo?

An echo is when you shout in a large empty hall or in a tunnel, and you hear the noise ringing back out at you a moment or two later. The echo is simply the sound of your voice bouncing back from the walls. You don't normally hear echoes, because they only bounce back clearly off smooth, hard surfaces – and in confined spaces. Even in a confined space, the wall must be at least 17 metres (55 ft) away, because you will hear an echo only if it bounces back at least 0.1 second after you shouted.

Long, low-frequency sound waves give low-pitched sounds.

Short, high-frequency sound waves give high-pitched sounds.

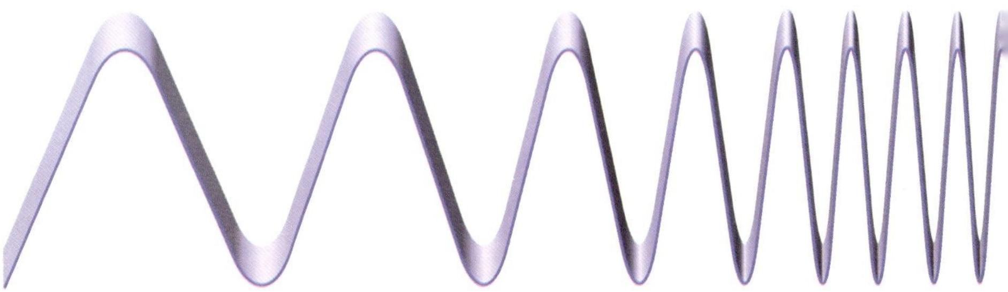

Index